ALL NEW
Crafts
for
Kwanzaa

KATHY ROSS
illustrated by Sharon Lane Holm

For
Mom and Dad
Happy
Kwanzaa!

M Millbrook Press   Minneapolis

In memory of Bear.

Text copyright © 2007 by Kathy Ross

Illustrations copyright © 2007 by Millbrook Press, Inc.

Millbrook Press, Inc.
A division of Lerner Publishing Group
241 First Avenue North
Minneapolis, Minnesota 55401 U.S.A.

Website address: www.lernerbooks.com

Library of Congress Cataloging-in-Publication Data

Ross, Kathy (Katharine Reynolds), 1948–
    All new crafts for Kwanzaa / Kathy Ross; illustrated by Sharon Lane Holm.
      p.   cm. — (All new holiday crafts for kids)
    ISBN 13: 978–0–7613–3401–9 (lib. bdg. : alk. paper)
    ISBN 10: 0–7613–3401–7 (lib. bdg. : alk. paper)
    1. Kwanzaa decorations. 2. Handicraft. I. Holm, Sharon Lane. II. Title. III. Series: Ross, Kathy (Katherine Reynolds), 1948- All-new holiday crafts for kids
    TT900.K92R66 2007
    745.594'1612—dc22   2005011059

Manufactured in the United States of America
1 2 3 4 5 6 – JR – 12 11 10 09 08 07

Contents

The *mkeka* is a mat on which the symbols of Kwanzaa are placed.

Woven Mat

Here is what you need:

seven 12-inch (30-cm) green pipe cleaners

eight 12-inch (30-cm) red pipe cleaners

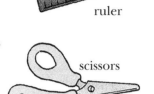
ruler

scissors

9- by 12-inch (23- by 30-cm) piece of black felt

red and green yarn

Here is what you do:

1 Fold the felt piece in half lengthwise. Cut eight 3-inch (8-cm) slits across the felt, making sure you do not cut all the way through to the edge of the felt.

2 Open up the felt piece. Starting with a red pipe cleaner, weave alternate red and green pipe cleaners into the felt to create the mat.

3 Fold the ends of the pipe cleaners under on each side of the mat, folding the edges of the felt over with the ends of the pipe cleaners.

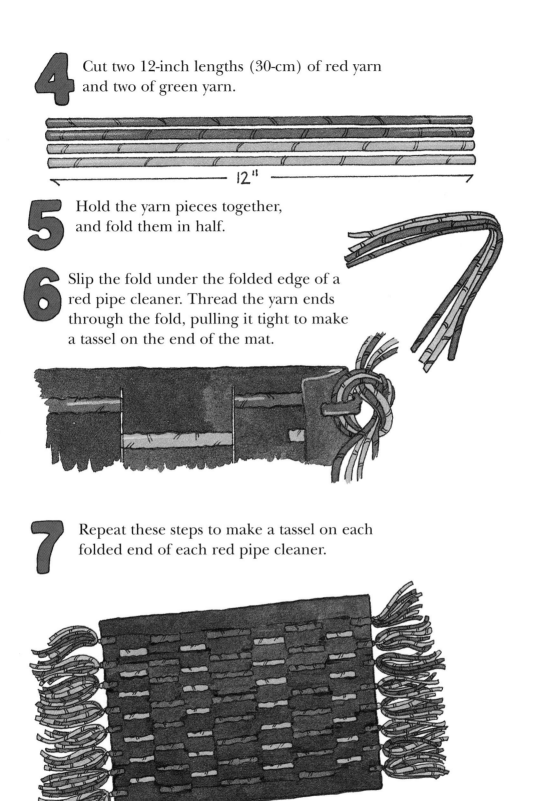

4 Cut two 12-inch lengths (30-cm) of red yarn and two of green yarn.

— 12" —

5 Hold the yarn pieces together, and fold them in half.

6 Slip the fold under the folded edge of a red pipe cleaner. Thread the yarn ends through the fold, pulling it tight to make a tassel on the end of the mat.

7 Repeat these steps to make a tassel on each folded end of each red pipe cleaner.

The mkeka represents the importance of history and tradition within the African-American family.

**The *kikombe cha umoja* is the big cup
that everyone drinks from at Kwanzaa time.**

Unity Cup

Here is what you need:

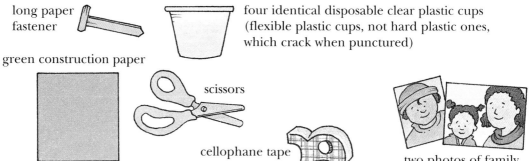

long paper
fastener

four identical disposable clear plastic cups
(flexible plastic cups, not hard plastic ones,
which crack when punctured)

green construction paper

scissors

cellophane tape

two photos of family
and friends

Here is what you do:

1 Make a paper to fit around the outside of one cup.
To do this, wrap a piece of construction paper
around the cup, and cut away the edges until it
is an exact fit.

2 Ask a grown-up to poke a small hole in the
center of the bottom of three of the cups.

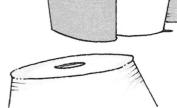

3 Trim the two photographs to fit on the
paper liner. Roll pieces of cellophane
tape, sticky side out, and attach the
photos to the liner. Make sure the
pictures will be right side up when the
cup is turned upside down.

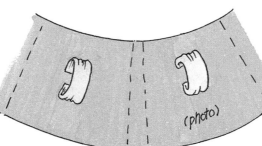

(photo)

6

4 Turn one cup with a hole in the bottom upside down. Put the liner with the photos on it around the cup, then slip a second cup with a hole over the first cup to secure the liner.

5 Take the third cup with a hole in the bottom, and set it, right side up, on the two upside-down cups.

6 Attach the cup to the bottom cups by putting the paper fastener through the holes in the three cups, bending the arms to opposite sides. Secure the fastener by covering the bent arms with cellophane tape.

7 Drop the last cup inside the top cup as a liner. It can be removed to wash or replace.

The kikombe cha umoja is a symbol of unity among black people.

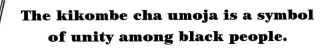

The seven principals of Kwanzaa are called the *nguzo saba*

Nguzo Saba Favor

Here is what you need:

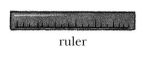
ruler

green and white
construction paper

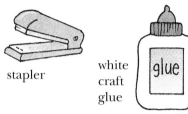
stapler

white
craft
glue

scissors

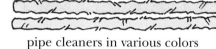
pipe cleaners in various colors

Here is what you do:

1 Cut a 2- by 5-inch (5- by 13-cm) strip of green construction paper.

2 Fold one narrow end over about ¼ inch (.06 cm) twice.

3 Staple the fold in the center to secure it.

4 Fold the opposite end over, and tuck it into the fold like you would a matchbook.

5 Cut a 13- by 1½-inch (33- by 4-cm) strip of white construction paper.

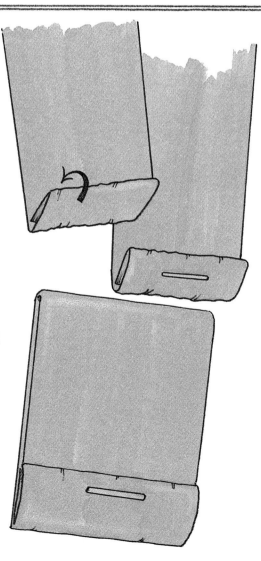

Fold the strip, accordion style, into seven folds to create eight sections.

 Glue the back section into the folder.

 Write "Nguzo Saba" on the front fold. Then pull the fold open, and write a different principal on each section.

 Roll a piece of pipe cleaner into a simple vegetable or fruit shape. Add details such as stems, leaves, or husks with pieces of pipe cleaner. Glue the fruit or vegetable to the front of the closed folder.

Nguzo Saba

Umoja
Kujichagulia
Ujima
Ujamaa
Nia
Kuumba
Imani

Nguzo Saba
The Seven Principles of Kwanzaa
Umoja (Unity)
Kujichagulia (Self-Determination)
Ujima (Collective Work and Responsiblity)
Ujamaa (Cooperative Economics)
Nia (Purpose)
Kuumba (Creativity)
Imani (Faith)

These little folders make meaningful Kwanzaa table favors. Make several in different colors, each with a different fruit or vegetable on the front.

Mazao, the fruits and vegetables, symbolize the fruit of all work.

Harvest Bowl Place Card

Here is what you need:

scissors

pony beads in assorted fruit and vegetable colors

glue

white craft glue

ruler

fabric scrap

soda bottle cap

toothpick

¾-inch (2-cm) flat button

rickrack

white and red construction paper

Here is what you do:

1 Cut two 2-inch (5-cm) squares from the fabric, and glue them together so the print is on the outside on both sides.

2 Glue the fabric square in the soda bottle cap.

2"

2"

3 Glue appropriate colors of beads into the cap to represent fruits and vegetables.

4 Trim away any excess fabric around the edges.

5 Cut a 2- by 3½-inch (5- by 9-cm) piece of white paper for the place card.

6 Cut a slightly larger piece of red paper to glue behind the white paper to form a border.

7 Glue the flat button in a corner of the white place card.

8 Glue two pony beads together to make the stand for the bowl.

9 Cut a piece of toothpick short enough to slip inside the two beads for added support. Dip the toothpick piece in glue, and slide it inside the two beads.

10 Glue the beads to the center of the button and the bowl on top of the beads.

11 Decorate the place cards with rickrack. Write a name on the card, positioning the bowl at the upper left.

Make a place card for each person at your Kwanzaa table, using different combinations of red, green, and black.

Munhindi **means corn and represents the children of the family.**

Corn Magnet

Here is what you need:

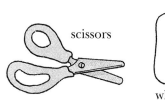
scissors

white craft glue

light cardboard

medium green rickrack

ruler

piece of sticky-back magnet

small yellow rickrack

Here is what you do:

1 Cut a 3- by 1-inch (8- by 2.5-cm) corn shape from the light cardboard.

2 Glue strips of yellow rickrack down the entire ear of corn to cover it.

3 Trim away the excess rickrack around the edge of the cardboard.

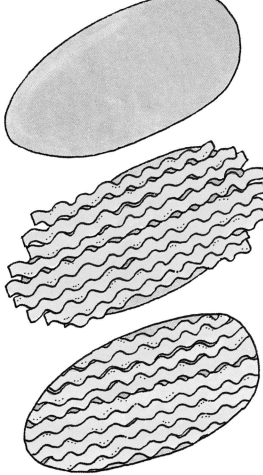

4 Cut six 3-inch (8-cm) pieces of the green rickrack.

— 3" —

5 Glue them on the two sides of the corn so they stick up from the back to look like the husks of the corn.

6 Press a piece of sticky-back magnet on the back of the corn.

Make an ear of corn magnet to represent each child in your family. What a great gift for your mom!

game
Tuesday
3:00

milk
cat food

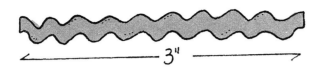

The candleholder is called the *kinara* and the seven candles
are called the *mishumaa saba*.

No-Fire Kwanzaa Candles

Here is what you need:

scissors

white craft glue

red, black, and
green pony beads

four 12-inch (30-cm) orange pipe cleaners

ruler

red, black, green, and white construction paper

brown felt

red and
green yarn

Here is what you do:

1 Make a frame for the candles by starting
with a 9- by 12-inch (23- by 30-cm) sheet of
red construction paper. Cut a black sheet
slightly smaller than the red, a green sheet
smaller than the black, and a white sheet
smaller than the green.

2 Glue the sheets together, from the
largest to the smallest, to
the green layer. Do not glue
the white piece on yet.

3 Cut a 24-inch (60-cm) piece of red
yarn and another of green yarn.
Hold them together, and slide
the ends behind the black
paper on each side to create
a hanger. Use additional glue
if needed.

14

Cut seven 6-inch (15-cm) orange pipe cleaners to make the flames.

 To make the candles, string nine red beads over three of the pipe-cleaner flames, nine green beads over each of three flames, and nine black beads over the last flame. The top of the pipe cleaners should barely be seen at the top of the candles.

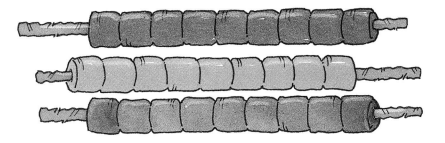

 Lay the bead candles, evenly spaced, along the white paper. Pick up each candle, and poke the pipe cleaner at the bottom through the paper so it is behind the paper and the candle is seen on the front of the paper. Trim off any pieces of pipe cleaner hanging below the bottom of the paper and fold in the sharp end.

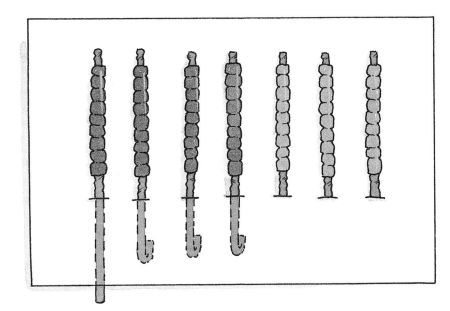

(continued on next page)

7 Glue the bead candles to the white sheet of paper. Be careful not to get any glue on the pipe cleaners.

8 Glue an 8- by 2-inch (20- by 5-cm) strip of brown felt across the base of the candles for a holder. Trim with strips of red and green yarn.

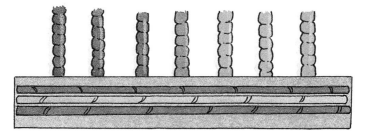

9 Glue the top edge and left side of the white paper to the center of the green paper on the frame.

To "light" each candle, push on the pipe-cleaner flame from behind the paper to make the flame come out on the top of the candle.

The *bendera*, or flag, is red, black, and green, the colors of Kwanzaa.

Bendera Notepad

Here is what you need:

white craft glue

scissors

red, green, and black felt

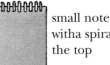

small notepad with a spiral at the top

pen

Here is what you do:

1 Rub glue all over the front and back covers of the notepad. Cover both sides of the notepad with one piece of black felt wrapped over the spiral.

2 Cut a red and a green felt strip for the front of the notepad that is one-third of the size of the front cover, lengthwise.

3 With the spiral on the left, glue the red strip to the top and the green strip to the bottom of the front cover to make the flag.

Slip the top part of a pen through the spiral wire to make a pole for the flag.

17

Zawadi means gifts.
The last day of Kwanzaa is a time for sharing zawadi.

Woven Corn Photo Card

Here is what you need:

yellow, black, red, and green
construction paper

ruler

photo of
you

marker

scissors

glue

white craft glue

brown lunch bag

Here is what you do:

1 Fold a 12- by 18-inch (30- by 46-cm) sheet of black construction paper in half, then in half again to make a card.

2 Cut a simple corn shape out of only the top layer of the front of the card.

3 Fold a 5- by 8-inch (13- by 20-cm) piece of yellow construction paper in half. Cut slits across the fold about ½ inch (1.25 cm) apart, being careful not to cut to the end of the paper.

4 Cut ½-inch wide (1.25-cm) strips of yellow paper. Weave the strips in and out of the cut yellow paper to make the woven corn kernels.

5 Glue the woven yellow paper behind the cutout corn shape on the front of the card.

6 Cut husks from the brown lunch bag to glue on each side of the corn.

7 Cut a piece of red paper slightly smaller than the inside of the card, and glue it in place.

8 Cut a green piece of paper slightly smaller than the red piece. Glue it over the red so it frames the green.

9 Glue your photo to the center of the green paper.

10 Use the marker to write a Kwanzaa greeting above the photo, and sign your name and the date below it.

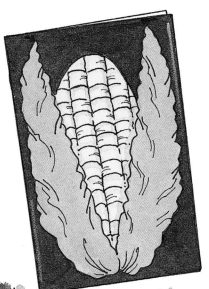

Make this card to give as a gift to someone who would love to have a picture of you!

If you are giving someone the gift of a book for Kwanzaa, you might want to make this bookmark to give with it.

Kwanzaa Bookmark

Here is what you need:

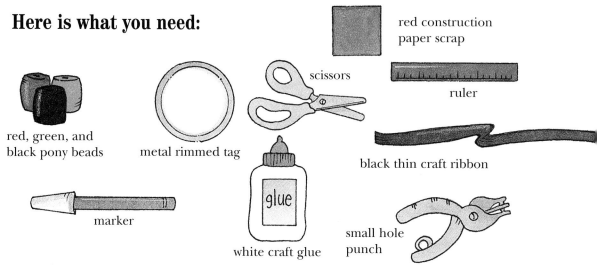

red, green, and black pony beads

metal rimmed tag

scissors

red construction paper scrap

ruler

black thin craft ribbon

marker

glue

white craft glue

small hole punch

Here is what you do:

 Using a marker, write a Kwanzaa message on one side of the tag.

 Use the hole punch to make a small hole in the tag below the message.

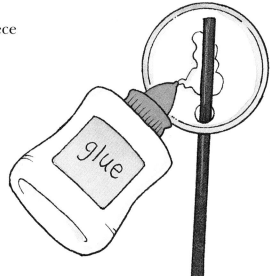
For Mom-
Kwanzaa!!
love Jay

 Cut a 12-inch long (30-cm) piece of black ribbon.

4 Thread one end of the ribbon through the hole, and secure it with glue on the back of the tag.

Cut a circle of red construction paper to glue over the back of the tag.

 Tie a double knot about 3 inches (8 cm) from the end of the ribbon.

7 String three beads, one of each color, on the ribbon to the knot, and tie a double knot below them.

To make the bookmark more personal, glue your photo to the back of the tag in place of the construction paper.

For Mom
Kwanzaa!!
love Jay

**Wow your friends and family
with this creative idea for a Kwanzaa favor.**

Corn Favor

Here is what you need:

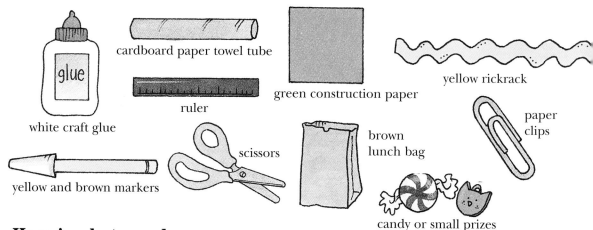

white craft glue

cardboard paper towel tube

ruler

green construction paper

yellow rickrack

paper clips

yellow and brown markers

scissors

brown lunch bag

candy or small prizes

Here is what you do:

1 Flatten one side of the tube, and fold the two sides in so that the end of the tube forms a point.

2 Secure the folds with glue. Hold them in place with paper clips until the glue has dried.

3 Cut a 2½-inch (6-cm) piece off the other end of the tube.

4 Cover the cut piece with green construction paper, and glue it down. Decorate the top and bottom edge with the yellow rickrack.

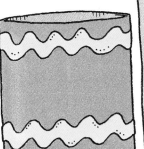

5 Fill the tube with candy or small prizes.

22

Shake the prizes down to the point of the tube. Flatten the open end, and glue it shut, holding it with paper clips until the glue is dry. Lay the tube flat so the candy or prizes stay away from the glued end until the glue is dry.

 Color the exposed area of the tube corn yellow with the marker. Use the brown marker to draw the kernels on the corn.

 Cut corn shucks from the brown lunch bag. Glue them on each side of the tube corn and around the back so they stick up behind the corn.

 Glue the end of the corn into the green tube.

Use the marker to write the name of the person the corn favor is for on the front of the tube.

Make a photo line to display pictures of family and friends.

Kwanzaa Photo Line

Here is what you need:

ruler

scissors

black, green, and red pony beads

package of red baby rickrack

large plastic-coated paper clips in red and green

glue

white craft glue

Here is what you do:

1 Cut a 5-foot (1.5 m) piece of rickrack for the photo line.

2 Fold an end into a loop, and glue it to create the hanger for one end.

3 Slide a red, green, and black pony bead over the loop to the end, and glue them in place.

4 Thread a red, green, and black pony bead on the rickrack, leaving space in between each group to hang a photo.

5 Glue the beads in place if you need to, but they will probably stay in place on their own on the rickrack.

6 Slide alternating red and green paper clips over the rickrack between each set of beads.

7 Finish the end in a loop with beads, just as you did the opposite end.

Hang the photo line by the loops, and attach photographs to it with the paper clips.

This bookmark is the perfect gift for a friend or sibling who needs help getting library books back on time.

Reminder Bookmark

Here is what you need:

envelope at least 7 inches (18 cm) wide

thin craft ribbon

white craft glue

ruler

marker

scissors

red, green, and black pony beads

green plastic berry basket

construction paper scraps

Here is what you do:

1 Cut a 2-inch wide (5-cm) strip off the bottom of the envelope. You can color the envelope if it is not already a color, or leave it white.

2 Cut a 4-inch long (10-cm) strip of plastic from the side of the berry basket. Make it narrower than the bookmark. Try to cut a strip that has a nice design to it. The design will depend on the basket you use, as they vary.

3 Cut a 24-inch (61-cm) piece of ribbon.

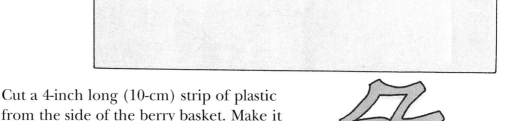

4 Weave an end of the ribbon through one side of the design, then over the end and down the other side.

 5 Pull the end of the ribbon so that the two ends hanging down are of equal length.

 6 Tie some pony beads on the ends of the ribbon.

 7 Glue the plastic to a scrap of construction paper in a color other than the color of the envelope.

 8 Trim the paper off around the plastic so that the paper forms a background for the plastic.

 9 Glue the paper-backed plastic to the bottom part of the envelope bookmark so that the ribbons hang down from the bottom.

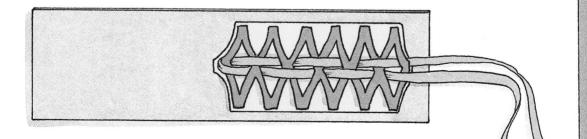

(continued on next page)

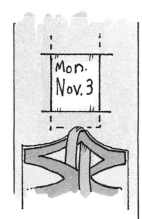

10 Cut two 1-inch (2.5-cm) slits on the right and left side above the plastic design through only the top layer of the envelope bookmark.

11 Cut several strips of paper to stack and slide into the slot.

12 Use the marker to write "This library book is due back on" above the stack of paper in the slots. The date the book is due can be written on the top paper in the slots and the paper discarded when the book is returned. This will expose a new sheet of paper to write the date due for another borrowed book.

The perfect gift for a reader!

Make snack dishes in the colors of Kwanzaa.

Kwanzaa Snack Dishes

Here is what you need:

disposable plastic plates
and containers

plastic lids and caps in
red, black, and green

white craft glue

trim

Here is what you do:

 Collect red, black, and green
plastic lids in a variety of
shapes and sizes.

2 Choose one red lid, one black lid,
and one green lid, and stack them
to make a base for the dish.

3 Glue the lids together.

4 Glue a plastic plate or container
on top of the lid base.

**To decorate, glue trim around
the edge of the plate or the
outside of the container.**

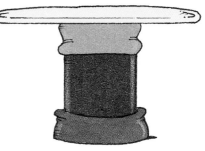

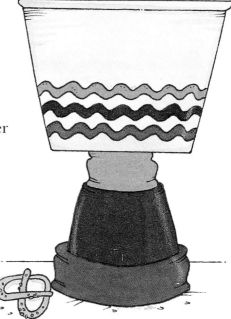

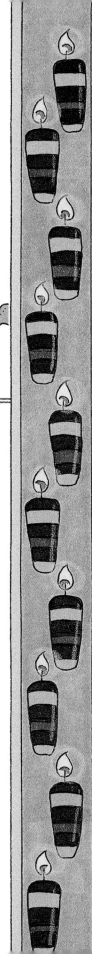

Make a pretty necklace in no time at all!

Wire Craft Necklace

Here is what you need:

scissors

white craft glue

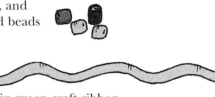
red, black, and green seed beads

thin green craft ribbon

ruler

small paper clip

pencil

Here is what you do:

1 Pull the paper clip open, and wrap it around a pencil to make a spiral.

2 Bend one end to make a hanger.

3 Thread seed beads on the spiral.

4 Secure the last few beads with glue.

5 Cut a 24-inch (60-cm) length of green ribbon.

6 Thread the spiral onto the ribbon and tie the ends together.

Red or black ribbon would also look very nice.

**This cuffed bracelet brings to mind
the beautiful beadwork done in Africa.**

Beaded Cuff Bracelet

Here is what you need:

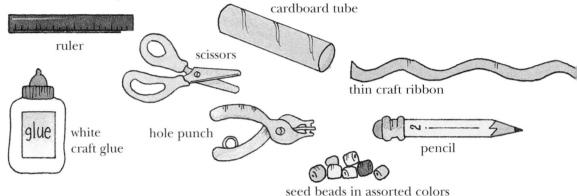

ruler

cardboard tube

scissors

thin craft ribbon

glue

white
craft glue

hole punch

pencil

seed beads in assorted colors

Here is what you do:

1 Cut a 1½-inch (4-cm) band
from the end of the cardboard tube.

2 Cut down the cardboard ring
to open it up on one side.

3 Use the hole punch to make a hole in the
center of the edge on each side of the cut.

4 Use the pencil to draw a simple
design on the side of the bracelet,
such as an ear of corn.

1½"

34

5 Color the design by gluing the correct color beads in each area.

6 When the design is complete, glue another color or colors of beads around the design to completely cover the outside of the bracelet.

7 Cut a 12-inch long (30-cm) piece of the ribbon. Thread an end through each hole in the cuff, and tie in a bow.

The ribbon tie allows the bracelet to adjust to a variety of wrist sizes.

Make this quick version of a beautiful African beaded doll.

Beaded Doll

Here is what you need:

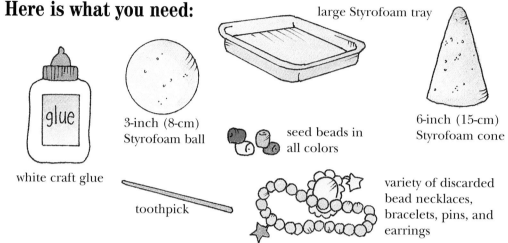

large Styrofoam tray

3-inch (8-cm) Styrofoam ball

seed beads in all colors

6-inch (15-cm) Styrofoam cone

white craft glue

toothpick

variety of discarded bead necklaces, bracelets, pins, and earrings

Here is what you do:

1 To make the body of the doll, cover the Styrofoam cone with glue, and wrap the entire cone with beaded necklaces. If any of the necklaces have clasps, press the clasps into the Styrofoam at the beginning and end of the wrap.

2 Sprinkle the body with seed beads to fill in any exposed Styrofoam. Do not put beads on the flat top of the cone where the head will be attached.

3 Cover the Styrofoam ball with glue.

4 Choose two identical earrings to press into the Styrofoam ball for the eyes. Choose a small stud earring for the nose and a curved earring for the mouth. Pierced earrings are easiest to use, but clamp earrings will also work. Just push the clamps into the Styrofoam.

5 Cover the back, top, and sides of the Styrofoam ball with jewels for hair.

6 Sprinkle the rest of the exposed area with seed beads.

7 Cover the flat top of the Styrofoam body with glue. Insert a toothpick in the center of the top.

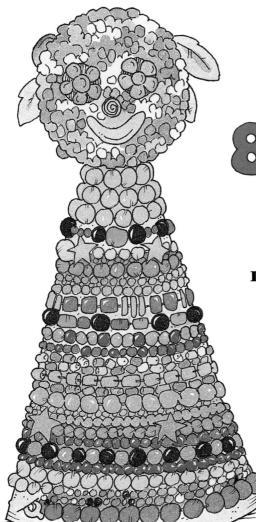

8 Press the head on the body over the toothpick.

Let the doll dry completely on the Styrofoam tray before picking it up.

Make these colorful coasters to use or to give as a gift

Harvest Coasters

Here is what you need:

scissors

white craft glue

disposable plastic plates in red and yellow (and other fruit and vegetable colors if you can find them)

green and brown felt

Here is what you do:

1 Cut simple rounded fruit and vegetable shapes from the flat part of the plastic plates. The red makes nice apples and tomatoes and the yellow makes nice pears. The shape must be large enough to place a glass on it.

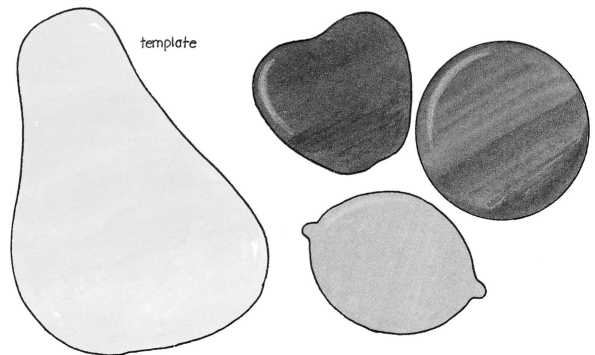
template

Cut around the shape on the green felt,leaving a border of felt that will show under the fruit or vegetable shape.

 Glue the shape to the felt.

 Cut a stem from the brown felt and a leaf, if appropriate, from the green felt. Glue them in place.

Make a variety of fruit and vegetable coasters based on the different colors of disposable plastic plates you have.

This idea will allow even the smallest child to "light" the Kwanzaa candles.

"Light the Candles" Kwanzaa Card

Here is what you need:

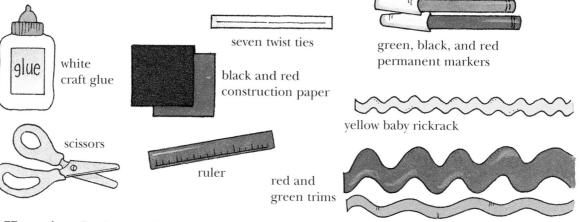

white craft glue

seven twist ties

black and red construction paper

green, black, and red permanent markers

scissors

ruler

red and green trims

yellow baby rickrack

Here is what you do:

1 Cut a 10- by 6-inch (25- by 15-cm) strip of black construction paper.

2 Fold it in half to make a card that opens at the bottom.

3 Trim the twist ties to 3½-inches (9 cm) long for the seven candles.

4 Fold ½-inch (1.25 cm) down at the top of each twist tie.

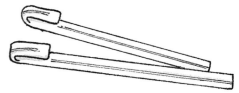

5 Color three twist ties green, three red, and one black, coloring over the folded part as well as the rest of each twist tie.

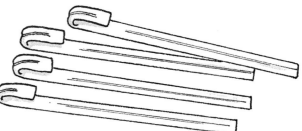

6 Glue the candles evenly spaced across the card with the three green ones on the left side, then the black one, and then the three red candles.

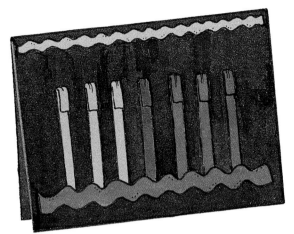

 7 Glue a strip of trim across the bottom of the card for the candleholder. Glue trim across the top of the card to add further decoration.

 8 Unfold the tops of the seven candles.

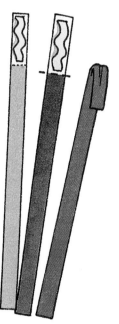

9 Cut a ½-inch (1.25-cm) piece of yellow rickrack to glue over the top of each candle for the flame.

 10 When the glue has dried, fold each flame down again so it is no longer visible.

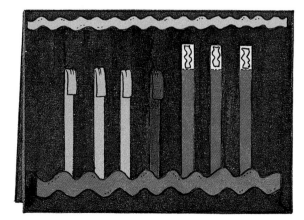

(continued on next page)

11 Glue a square of red construction paper inside the card.

12 Use the marker to write a Kwanzaa greeting and sign your name.

Happy Kwanzaa! love, Tyrone

To "light" the candles just unfold the top of the candle to show the flame.

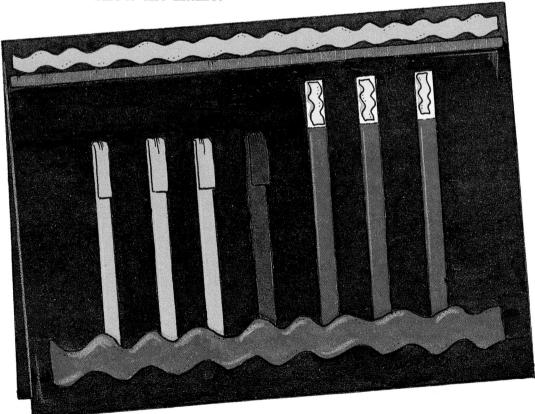

Make a unity cup to wear!

Wooden Cup Pin

Here is what you need:

brown permanent marker

wooden ice-cream spoon

scissors

pin back

white craft glue

glue

brown rickrack

Here is what you do:

1 Use scissors to cut a 1-inch (2.5-cm) piece off the handle end of the wooden spoon and a ½-inch (1.25-cm) piece off the spoon end.

2 Use the brown marker to color the remainder of the spoon and the piece cut from the spoon end.

3 Glue the top of the rounded tip behind the narrow end of the remaining spoon piece to form the base of the cup.

4 Glue a pin back to the back of the cup.

5 Glue brown rickrack trim across the top of the cup and the seam at the base where he two pieces are joined together to represent a carved design in the wood.

Can you think of a way to decorate the cup to look like the *kikombe cha umoja* at your house?

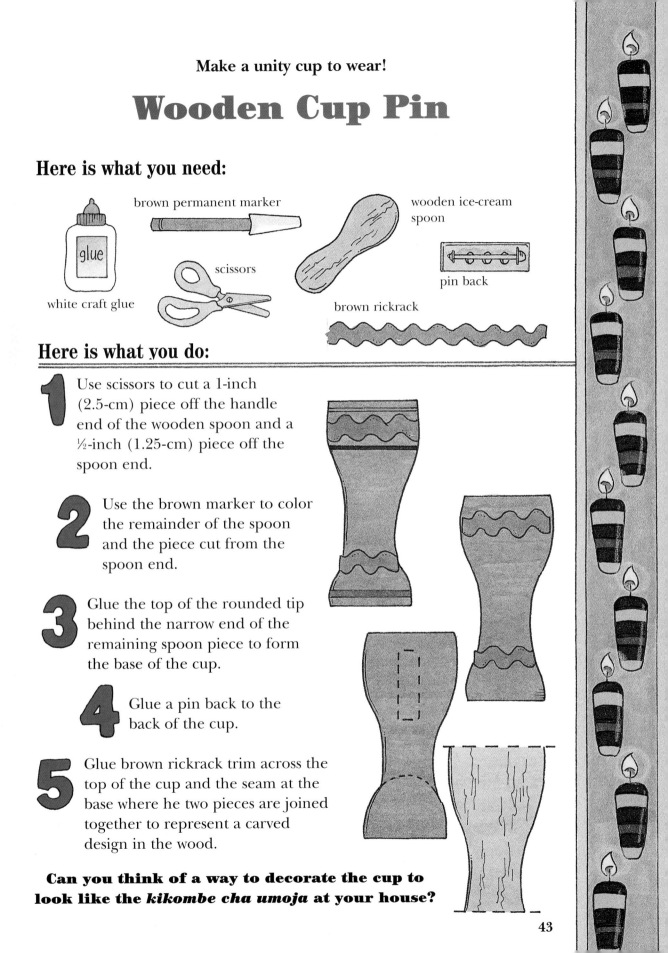

This rhythm instrument is based on the African nut hulls shakers.

Nut Hulls Shaker

Here is what you need:

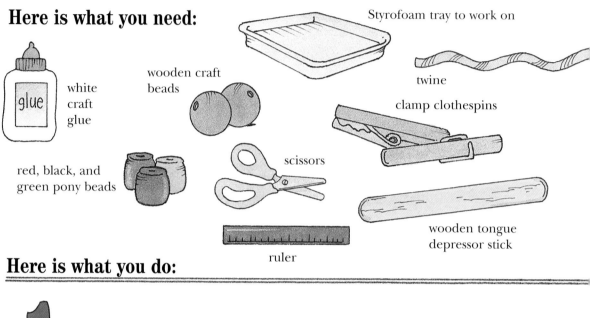

Styrofoam tray to work on

white craft glue

wooden craft beads

twine

clamp clothespins

red, black, and green pony beads

scissors

wooden tongue depressor stick

ruler

Here is what you do:

1 Cut ten 12-inch long (30-cm) pieces of twine.

12"

2 Tie a wooden craft bead to the end of each piece of twine. Secure the knot with a dab of glue.

3 Cover one side of the wooden stick with glue.

4 Place the twine on the glue so that the beads are about 2 inches (5 cm) from one end of the stick and the ends of the strings hang down from the opposite end of the stick.

5 Cover the twine and the opposite side of the stick with glue.

6 Wrap the entire stick with twine, securing both ends with glue. Secure the ends with clamp clothespins, if needed, until the glue has dried. Let the project dry completely on the Styrofoam tray.

7 Tie some pony beads to the loose ends of twine hanging down below the stick.

Shake the rhythm stick in time to your favorite music.

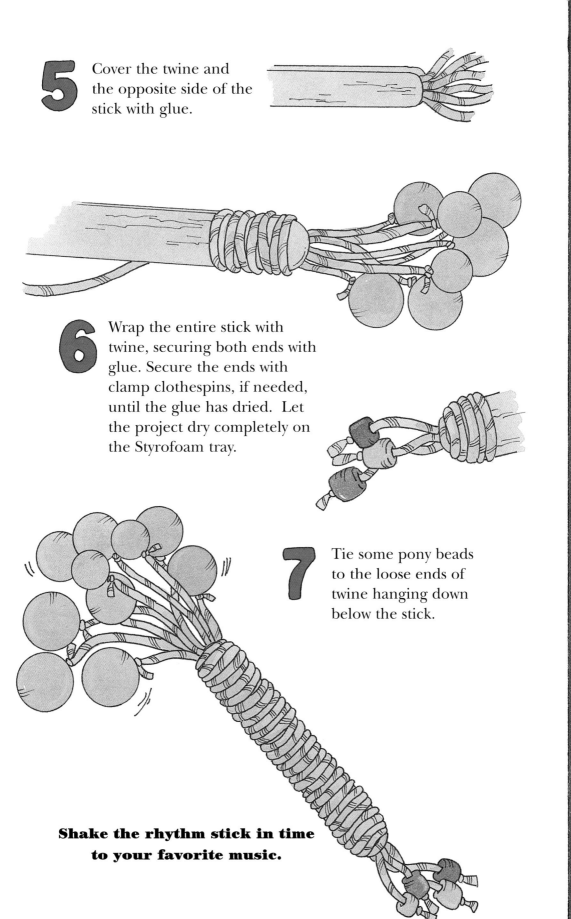

Your Kwanzaa guests will be surprised to discover this drum is edible!

Cookie Drum Favor

Here is what you need:

marker

ruler

brown construction paper

red, black, and green pony beads

scissors

twine

hole punch

cellophane tape

three sandwich-type cookies or five to six single cookies

Here is what you do:

1 Stack the cookies.

2 Cut two identical brown paper circles that are slightly larger around than the cookies.

3 Hold the two brown circles together, and use the hole punch to make holes around the outside.

4 Cut a 3-foot (1-m) piece of twine.

5 Hold the stack of cookies with a paper circle on the top and one on the bottom. Thread the twine through a hole leaving a 6-inch (15-cm) tail to use at the end to tie the twine ends together.

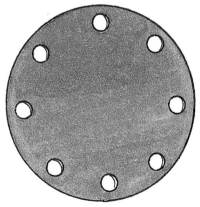
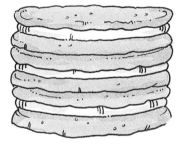

Thread the twine down through the hole in the bottom paper circle that is opposite the top hole you started with. Continue to thread the twine up and down through the holes until the top and bottom circles have been sewn together over the cookies to look like a drum.

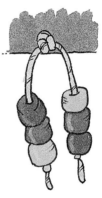

 Tighten the twine, beingcareful not to tear throughthe holes. If you do tear ahole, repair it with a piece of cellophane tape.

 Tie the ends of the twine together to secure them. Thread some pony beads on each end of the twine, and knot to keep them from slipping off. Trim off any excess twine.

You can write the name of the person the drum is for on the top of the drum.

About the Author and Artist

Thirty years as a teacher and director of nursery school programs have given Kathy Ross extensive experience in guiding young children through craft projects. Among the more than forty craft books she has written are *Crafts for All Seasons*, *All Girl Crafts*, *The Scrapbooker's Idea Book*, *Things to Make for Your Doll*, and *Star-Spangled Crafts*. To find out more about Kathy, visit her website: www.Kathyross.com.

Sharon Lane Holm, a resident of Fairfield, Connecticut, won awards for her work in advertising design before shifting her concentration to children's books. Her recent books include *Happy New Year, Everywhere!* and *Merry Christmas, Everywhere!*, by Arlene Erlbach. You can see more of her work at www.sharonholm.com.

Together, Kathy Ross and Sharon Lane Holm have created *The Best Christmas Crafts Ever!* and *The Big Book of Christian Crafts*, as well as four earlier books in this series: *All New Crafts for Easter*, *All New Crafts for Thanksgiving*, *All New Crafts for Earth Day*, and *All New Crafts for Halloween*.

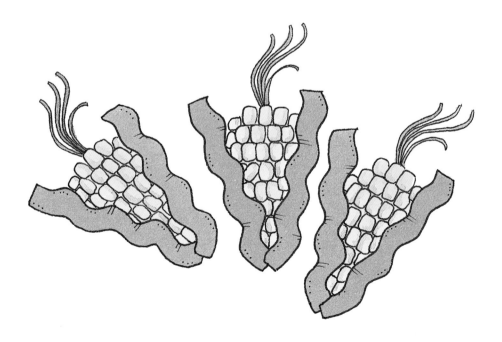